Letter's To My Future Wife
365 Days Of Undying Devotion

Anthony D. Green

Copyright © 2014 Anthony D. Green

All rights reserved.

ISBN-13:

978-0692315316 (Love's Signature)

ISBN-10:

0692315314

DEDICATION

This book is dedicated to all those who search for love effortlessly. Your search is not in vain. There is someone being created imperfectly perfect for you. Sometimes you just have to go through the storm in order to appreciate the sunny days that are ahead of you. If there's one thing I can say to you it's this.... Love like it was an accident, expect nothing but hope for everything. The best things in life are those things that are unexpected. It's in the unknown that you find the most beautiful things. So this book is dedicated to LOVE... Where it all begins...

Letter's To My Future Wife

ACKNOWLEDGMENTS

First and foremost I have to give honor to God. Words can't describe the humbleness that I have right now. I walked this earth for so long unsure of what it was that I was supposed to be doing and for so long I was rebellious to the calling you placed on my life. At times I ventured out trying to do things on my own. Felt like you had abandoned me at the time I needed you most but I realize now more than ever your footprints always walked beside me and at times the were the only ones in the sand while you carried me. I give you the glory for all that you have done and will do. Without you there would definitely be no me. I thank you for the gift that you bestowed on me as a writer. I thank you for my struggles, because in those struggles it brought me closer to you. If it weren't for those struggles I would not have found my purpose. I give you the praise each and every day Lord. I will yell it to the heavens daily......Thank You

To my family, the ones who keep my heart beating, keep the laughs coming, and the support flowing I thank you. I couldn't have asked for a better family. We are a huge family but the love matches that amount of members in my family. Thank you for being that extra push at times. For the harsh words that actually motivated me to do better. For the hugs when they were needed. For the places to stay, the food to eat, and the many great times that we have shared. If there's one thing that we know how to do it's party. Regardless of the occasion we find a reason to turn some music on and party. For everything you guys have ever done for me, from the bottom of my heart I thank you... You are one of the main reasons I do this. So to the Greens, Woods, Johnsons, Cunnigham, Thomas, Whitten, Edwards, Triplett, Whaleys, Williams, LeSure, Heath, Tillis, Kelly, Ruffin, McDaniel, Pettis, Martin, Stinson, Patton, Herman, House, & all I forgot to mention because it's a lot of us..... Thank you
~Family First~

To my Father George Green:
Dad I can't begin to tell you how much I love you. You are a walking testimony of what God can do in a man's life. I have watched him do some great things in your life. You are more than my father, you are my best friend. The one I can go to when I'm hurting and know that some way everything will make sense. It is because of you that I am who I am. You have always been my guiding light when I feel lost. I have watched you take care of your children with no regard to your own health. Work three job just to make sure we had everything we needed. You would go without just so we could have. You've missed countless hours of sleeping doctoring on us when we were sick, playing with us when we were bored, just being an all around father. I have had 30 great years on this earth with you and I look forward to many more. The were father doesn't equate to the man you have been for me. I could write a whole book on you and it still wouldn't explain the love I hold for you. I do this for you. I told you that one day I would make you proud of me and every day I have worked on doing just that. For everything you have done and continue to do I thank you and I love you so much.

To my Mother Alfreda Johnson
I am so in love with you. You have no idea just what you mean to me.   have seen you go through so much in your life. But through it all you found your way. You are the one woman that can never be replaced. I thank God for everything he delivered you from. You are my inspiration. May 8th 2006 was the hardest day for me, and from that day forward I made a promise to never break your heart again. Everything I am is because of you. You are the air I breath and the reason my heart continues to beat. I thank God daily for you. You are the closest image of God for me. No matter what happens in life know that I am so proud of you. You have become everything you were destined to be. There was a point where I thought that I had lost you. I fell to my knees and begged God not to take you from me. He answered my prayer because you are still with me. He has given me another chance to love you and take care

of you. I do this for you momma. I don't feel like I have given you the proper acknowledgement. Even this book isn't enough for me. I know at times I get so busy that it may feel like I have forgotten about you. Just know that I haven't. Each time my heart beats it's a reminder of who it beats for.... I love you momma

To Danine Ballard & Theresa Harrington:
I looked for the best definition of best friend. I found one in the Urban Dictionary that I actually like. "Best Friends are very special people in your life. They are the first people you think about when you make plans. They are the first people you go to when you need someone to talk to. You will phone them up just to talk about nothing, or the most important things in your life. When you're sad they will try their hardest to cheer you up. They give the best hugs in the world! They are the shoulder to cry on, because you know that they truly care about you. In most cases they would take a bullet for you, because it would be too painful to watch you get hurt." In my opinion this definition describes the both of you completely. I have watched you guys dang near fight for me. You have been in my corner supporting me all the way. You believe in my when I don't believe in myself. Danine I thank you for the past few months. You have stepped up more than most and done some things that I will forever be grateful for. I can't say thank you enough. Theresa each and every time I dialed your number you always answered and the first thing out your mouth was " Hey baby, is everything ok?" I can't tell you how good it feels to have someone that always is concerned about my well being. Each and every time I needed you ladies you were there. You never asked questions, you just had my back. I can't begin to tell you how much I need that in my life. Thank you

To Marie Christman

The other half to my creative process and thoughts. You are more than just a friend. Lately you have been my counselor, comforter, protector, stern voice, and so much more. I thank you for all the help you have given me in the completion of this book but more than that I thank you for being in my life at the point where your presence is needed more than anything. You are more that a reason or a season for me. I pray that the bond we share last a lifetime. I will always love you til there's no breath left in me and even then.

To India Bunch

From the moment you met me you said to me there was a reason we met each other. You were absolutely right about that. If it wasn't for that one conversation we had I wouldn't have found the push to write this book. You told me that I had a story to tell and so many needed to hear it. From those very words I went to work. You came into my life immediately as a protector. You can sense when something is wrong and you are there to offer the comfort needed.

You told me in my pain I would find purpose. That's why it's inscribe in my book. I tell myself this same thing daily. I can honestly say that I have found my purpose now. All the pain I have endured was for a much greater purpose than I could've imagined.

My spirit is made whole now. The broken pieces of my life and being pieced together perfectly. Thank you for everything you said, did, and simply for being you. My lioness and my protector as you have rightfully so named yourself....

To Anthony "AJ" Jones

Man I already told you that you were more than my barber. In the past few years of knowing you I can honestly say that you have grown to be my brother. I am grateful to have someone like you in my life for guidance, good laughs, and a great haircut. As long as I'm walking this earth AJ Styles Barber and Beauty Salon 42 w Lake Street in Oak Park will always be my second home.

To Morris "Moe-Mentum" Garrett

Every man needs a man to look up to. You are that man for me. You have been my mentor since I stepped on the scene. You took me under your wing and developed me into a great poet as well as a man. Thank you for being that big brother I needed. You told me my gift will make room for me and it's doing just that. I am looking forward to your book.

To Areka Danae

In the past few months you have made such an impact on me. You came in and fell right into my craziness and brought a good amount of your own into my world. I love you for that. You don't try hard but with minimal effort you love my crazy self. I have cried several times on your shoulder and you have been there to save me from my feelings. I hope that this friendship last a lifetime. Just know no matter where I go I will love you always

To Lashonda Edwards

Through the years the one thing that hasn't changed is the love you have for me. You are still here and for that reason I thank God daily for you. The funny thing is we don't have to see each other every day to know that there is something there that won't ever change. You know my heart, my deepest darkest secrets, and everything that makes me me and you protect my heart daily. If there's one thing that will never change it's my undying love for you. I will always love you

To Tiffany Fairchild

Words can't express the love I hold for you. From that very first day you walked into my life I have loved you. You have shown me the real meaning of an unconditional love without physical interactions. You have always been there arms open ready to offer me whatever I needed. That's so hard to come by but I am grateful I have that in you. Know that distance could never keep us away from each other. I carry you in my heart everywhere I go. I love you bff...

To Chanel Bean

It's funny how you came into my life. But it's not coincidence that you have made your presence know in so many ways. You are my mental counterpart, at times my teacher, my daily inebriation, my listening ear, my comforter, and most importantly you have managed to become a very good friend of mine. But that's not where our story ends. In a split second you managed to do something that I have never experienced in 30 years on this earth. Each day you are around is a constant reminder that prayer really does work and having faith the size of a mustard seed can produce great things. I look forward to the masterpiece we create together. I look forward to the journey we embark on together. But most importantly I look forward to you. You are the mere reflection of everything that I write and pray for daily and I am fortunate to share any moment with you. You have tapped into a place that I swore sacred. You find the very essence of me and every chance you get you help me discover me. I am a better man because of you. I thank you for every call, every conversation, every hug, every smile, and most importantly I thank you for simply being you. For everything I am and everything I will be from this moment forward I say thank you in advance......

To my Poetic Family and Friends

We have a bond that has definitely stood the test of time. You are my extended family in every way possible. We have shared stages, tears, laughs, meal, and so much more together. I am so grateful for all the support that I have received from each and every one of you. There are so many things I take from a family like you all. To my poetic sisters Tierra Clark, Shameeka Shavers, Courtney Nyree, Nicole Paschal, Tiffany Henderson, Tamisha 4'11 Collins, Evie Wells, Danielle Barnhart, Angela "Imani Truth" Mason, Terri "Lyric"Green, Drina "Love Is" Johnson, C. Morson, Dorene Morrow, Lyrical Paradigm, Robin Bobo, Deana Dean, Shettima "Mocha" Webb, Alicia "Restore" Spikes, Kendria "K Love" Harris, Taletha Wallace, Tia Crayton, Brenda Matthews, Jhenna Beckles, Jarita Steward, Mimi Marmalade, Drina "Love Is" Johnson, Toly

Walker, Sable Nerette, Alyssa Devin, Lah Marshall, Robyn Shanae, Awthentik, and so many other great women. You ladies have been inspiration for me through this journey in so many ways. To my poetic brothers Ollie Woods, Jeronimo, Terrence Ellery, Black Diamond, Blaq Ice, Poetry Soulchild, Brainstorm, Odyssey, Jason Williams, Ben Ammi Israel, Tim Henry, & Kwabena Nixon.

Day 1

Dear Future Wife:

I woke up today and I really missed you. It seems like everywhere I turn I see your face. I went to my place of serenity to find peace with you but your scent lingered in the air. I realize that there's no escaping this feeling. I'm eagerly awaiting your arrival because my days have been lonely without you here. But I know in the end we will be together. So I find peace in that till I can find peace in you. I love you.....

Yours truly,

Your Future Husband

Day 2

Dear Future Wife

I dreamt of you last night. Funny thing is I dream of you every night these days. You have found a way to occupy my mind in the loneliest moments. I wake up still feeling your head on my chest and in that moment I miss you more than ever. How can this be? How can I miss someone that isn't mine? I've yet to find the answer to this question but I'm sure you'll answer it for me. I look forward to that day our eyes meet. I long to feel you in my arms. Then and only then will all this make sense. I hope that wherever you are you're missing me as much as I'm missing you. I Love You.....

Forever Yours

Your Future Husband

DAY 3

DEAR FUTURE WIFE

TODAY FEELS A LITTLE BETTER. WOKE UP THINKING ABOUT YOU AND HOW IT'S GOING TO FEEL TO WAKE UP TO YOU. YOUR EYES, YOUR SMILE, AND THE SWEETEST MORNING BREATH I'VE EVER SMELLED. HEARING THAT ANGELIC VOICE OF YOURS SAY GOOD MORNING AS YOU LEAN OVER TO KISS ME. SWEAR I CAN FEEL YOUR HAND STROKING MY FACE. IT WOULD BE A FIGHT TO GET OUT OF BED SO I SEE US HAVING COUNTLESS HOURS LOST THERE. BUT IT WOULD BE WORTH IT BECAUSE FINALLY I'D HAVE YOU. I LOVE YOU....

YOURS FOREVER

YOUR FUTURE HUSBAND

Day 4

DEAR FUTURE WIFE:

DO YOU DREAM OF FOREVER LIKE I DO? I'VE DREAMT OF THE PERFECT LOCATION, THE ALTER, ME IN MY TUX, BUT THE ONE THING I HAVEN'T SEEN IS U. I WONDER WHAT YOU'LL LOOK LIKE. HOW BEAUTIFUL YOU'LL BE WALKING DOWN THAT AISLE, YOUR SMILE, AND THAT AMAZING DRESS YOU'LL HAVE ON. WORDS CAN'T DESCRIBE THE JOY I'D FEEL FROM THAT MOMENT AND EVERY MOMENT AFTER. DO YOU EVER WONDER WHAT FOREVER FEELS LIKE? I IMAGINE WE BOTH SIT AND THINK ABOUT IT AT THE SAME TIME. MAYBE THAT'S WHY AT THAT MOMENT I FEEL COMPLETE. I WISH U WERE HERE. THERE'S SO MUCH I WANT TO TELL YOU. BUT I KNOW GOD IS PREPARING US FOR THOSE VERY MOMENTS. TIL THEN I'LL CONTINUE TO LAY HERE AND DREAM OF YOU. I LOVE YOU

FOREVER YOURS

YOUR FUTURE HUSBAND

DAY 5

DEAR FUTURE WIFE:

WHAT'S YOUR DEFINITION OF FOREVER? PEOPLE USE THAT WORD SO LOOSELY THESE DAYS. FOR ME FOREVER DOESN'T EQUATE TO WHAT I WANT TO SHARE WITH YOU. I'VE SEARCHED FOR THE APPROPRIATE WORD AND HAVE COME UP WITH ONLY ONE "ETERNAL". THE UNBREAKABLE BOND BETWEEN TWO SOULMATES DESTINED FOR EACH OTHER... THAT'S THE KIND OF LOVE I WANT US TO HAVE.... THAT ETERNAL LOVE... AN ENDLESS, NEVER ENDING, UNWAVERING, NEVER CHANGING, UNBREAKABLE LOVE. THIS IS WHAT I WILL OFFER YOU THE DAY WE SAY " I DO". I LOVE YOU.

FOREVER YOURS,

YOUR FUTURE HUSBAND

DAY 6

DEAR FUTURE WIFE

TODAY THE VOID OF NOT HAVING YOU HERE HAS ME FEELING SOME TYPE OF WAY. YOU DON'T KNOW HOW MUCH I PRAY THAT GOD REVEALS WHO YOU ARE. BUT SEEING THAT HE HASN'T YET TELLS ME THAT IT'S NOT TIME. DO YOU FEEL LIKE I DO? DO YOU YEARN TO FEEL MY TOUCH? DO YOU WAKE UP MISSING ME? DO YOU WONDER WHAT MY KISS WOULD FEEL LIKE? THESE THOUGHTS THAT RACE THROUGH MY MIND KEEP ME WONDERING WHAT THE FUTURE HOLDS FOR US. THERE'S SO MUCH I DON'T KNOW BUT THE ONE THING I'M VERY CERTAIN OF IS I HAVE SO MUCH LOVE I'M READY TO GIVE TO YOU. I'M READY TO LEARN JUST WHAT IT TAKES TO HAVE A TASTE OF FOREVER. I LOOK BACK OVER MY LIFE AND I SEE THE MISTAKES I'VE MADE AND I KNOW ONE THING IS FOR CERTAIN I'LL NEVER MAKE THE SAME MISTAKES AGAIN. I'M PREPARING MYSELF FOR YOU. I'M GETTING READY FOR THAT DAY OUR HEARTS BECOME ONE. I SEE SO MANY OTHERS EXPERIENCING WHAT IS MEANT FOR US. I SMILE BECAUSE I KNOW OUR TIME IS COMING. TIL THEN JUST KNOW I'M ALWAYS THINKING ABOUT YOU. I LOVE YOU

WITH ALL MY LOVE

YOUR FUTURE HUSBAND

Day 7

DEAR FUTURE WIFE:

THE SEARCH FOR YOU HAS BEEN HARD. I CAN'T BEGIN TO TELL YOU THE EMOTIONS I GO THROUGH EVERY DAY. I SIT HERE AND THINK ABOUT WHEN DID ALL THIS START. WHEN DID I DECIDE THAT I WANTED A WIFE. THE ANSWER TO THAT IS SINCE I WAS A KID. I CAN'T BEGIN TO TELL YOU THE THOUGHTS I HAD ABOUT MARRIAGE EVEN BEFORE I KNEW WHAT LOVE REALLY WAS OR UNDERSTOOD WHAT IT MEANT TO HAVE A WIFE BUT I DESIRED IT NONETHELESS. TO ME THAT IS COMPLETION... A BEAUTIFUL END TO WHAT SEEMS LIKE A NEVER ENDING BATTLE. I SEE SO MANY OF THE WRONG REPRESENTATIONS OF WHAT A MARRIAGE SHOULD BE AND IT HURTS BECAUSE PEOPLE DON'T REALLY UNDERSTAND LOVE. I FIND MYSELF AT TIMES ANGRY AT THOSE WHO HAVE THE OPPORTUNITY TO HAVE SOMEONE THEY CAN SPEND THEIR LIFE WITH AND ABUSE IT. THEY MAKE IT SEEM SO MEANINGLESS BUT TO ME IT MEANS EVERYTHING. I AM WELL AWARE THAT THERE WILL BE PROBLEMS, THAT THE ROAD WILL NOT ALWAYS BE AN EASY ONE, THAT AT TIMES WE BOTH WILL FALL SHORT, THAT THERE WILL BE MANY BATTLES WE WILL HAVE TO FIGHT BUT I FEEL THAT AS LONG AS WE FIGHT THEM TOGETHER WE CAN MAKE IT THROUGH. I COULD NEVER TREAT YOU LIKE A SECRET OR SOMETHING THAT THE WORLD WILL NEVER KNOW OF. HOW COULD THE BEST PART OF MY LIFE BE THAT? I WOULD YELL IT FROM THE TOP OF THE TALLEST BUILDING BECAUSE THAT'S HOW YOU'D MAKE ME FEEL... LIKE I'M ON TOP OF THE WORLD. NOTHING OR NO ONE WOULD COME BEFORE YOU AND THE VALIDITY OF OR RELATIONSHIP WILL ALWAYS STAY STRONG. IN THIS WAIT FOR YOU I AM LEARNING SO MUCH ABOUT MYSELF AND I'M WORKING ON THOSE THINGS TO BE THE CLOSEST THING TO PERFECTION FOR YOU. I WILL CONTINUE TO FIND WAYS TO RECREATE MYSELF SO THAT YOU CAN NEVER GET BORED WITH ME AND EVERY DAY I WOULD TELL YOU JUST HOW LUCKY I AM TO HAVE YOU. TO SOME WHAT I'M SAYING ARE JUST WORDS BUT TO ME IT'S MY PROMISE!! I PROMISE TO LOVE YOU LIKE

THAT WAS THE ONLY THING I WAS EVER GOOD AT. I PROMISE TO WALK WITH YOU EVERY STEP OF THE WAY. I PROMISE TO HOLD YOU WHEN YOU JUST NEED TO BE HELD. I PROMISE TO KISS YOU WHEN YOU NEED TO BE KISSED. I PROMISE TO LISTEN TO YOU EVERY TIME YOU NEED TO TALK. I COULD SIT HERE AND WRITE OUT EACH AND EVERY PROMISE BUT I WON'T. I'LL JUST SAY THAT I'LL DEVOTE EACH AND EVERY DAY TO MAKING SURE YOU NEVER REGRET WHAT WE HAVE. NEXT TO GOD YOU ARE ALL I'LL EVER NEED. I LOVE YOU.....

PATIENTLY WAITING,

YOUR FUTURE HUSBAND

Day 8

Dear Future Wife:

Today is one of those days that the desire for you is strong. I wake up feeling empty without u. It's like I can feel your presence but I can't physically see you. I know you're out there waiting for me. But it's days like this that your hug is needed more than ever. I never understood how powerful a hug could be till I no longer felt them. No other embrace is like yours. In your arms you offer comfort, protection, affection, admiration, serenity, sanctuary, and most importantly love. I need to feel this so bad. Waking up without you is becoming harder by the day. You have invaded my dreams in such a way that once I realize it's just a dream my heart hurts and I miss you. I have to cry internally because you're not here to wipe them if they should fall. I know they say patience is a virtue but I question just how patient the person was who made that statement. Did that person yearn to spend their life with someone. Did they wake up feeling this presence on their chest as if someone laid there the night before. Did everything remind them of what they didn't have but desired. I know as a man I'm supposed to be built Ford tough but I'm transparent when it comes to you. You're not a want for me, you're a need. Like I need to breathe I need you to feel complete and only you can give me that. Until that can happen I'll place my tears in these letters. I miss you and I Love You....

Yours Forever

Your Future Husband

Day 9

Dear Future Wife

It's days like this that I hurt more than any other days. Your side of the bed is empty. Pillow still smells like the fabric softener it was washed in when it should smell like you. I lay here and stare at that spot and imagine you laying there. The shape of your face, the sounds you'd make as you slept. I don't think I would get an ounce of sleep those first few nights because I would be so amazed to have you laying next to me. It's cold without you. I need your body next to me. I need to feel you wrapped in my arms. Why do I have to lay here without you. I'm tired of just dreaming about you. But I guess I should be grateful for those dreams of you. Are you thinking of me right now? Is your mind wandering the same things I am? It's so frustrating not knowing what the future holds for us. My mind plays out so many scenarios and I find joy in those thoughts. But sometimes the reality is more painful than the thoughts. I can't begin to tell you how much I yearn for you. How my heart beats for you but the rhythm is a little off right now. I hope that wherever you are you know that I love you. I pray you rest well and I miss you. I'm going to that place where we can be together. I'll see you soon.

Truly yours

Your Future Husband

Day 10

Dear Future Wife:

As I stare at this empty screen I smile. It's crazy because an empty screen for me means that something beautiful is about to be written. I can't begin to tell you how much you inspire me. Before the thought of you words were just well constructed letters of the alphabet but now they carry so much meaning. You did that for me. You have given me more reasons to write than I could've ever imagined having. There's so much I want to tell you that is going on in my life. So many things are coming together for me that I had no idea would. It's hard not having you here to share in these moments with me. It's like I can feel your presence but I can't see you. I can't touch you, hug you, kiss you or see that beautiful smile of yours that I yearn to see so bad. I know it's going to be the most captivating smile. I'm so ready to fall in love with you. To experience that feeling of free falling without ever worrying about hitting the ground because I know you'd be right there to catch me. Everything I am becoming is because of you. I can't tell you how your absence is preparing me for your arrival. How I'm building this empire for the two of us to share. So when you come I'll be ready. I picture that day. I imagine what I would say and how nervous I'd be. The way you'd look at me as I begin telling you how I've been praying for you before I even knew who you were. How I've already dreamt of how your hugs would feel and how your kisses would complete me. You have no idea the things I have in store for you. I'll leave you with this....forever isn't long enough to love you because it feels like that's how long I've waited. But I'll devote everyday to making it feel like eternity. That's my promise. I love you so much

Your Future Husband

Day 11

Dear Future Wife:

I find myself at times lost, unsure, and confused

There have been so many times I didn't know what to do

Then I look at you and that all changed

You saw my pain; you've felt the same,

you've lost when you wanted to gain.

so much about our life is the same

that's why this moment is so perfect

you found a way to love me past my surface

that's why these feelings surfaced so easily

you believe in me before actions come

you stay with me when it's so easy to run

I can't begin to tell you

all the things you've done

I can't tell you how I wake each morning before the sun rises

look at you in silence and scream thank you inside my head

that's why I'll pull you closer in bed

I don't want you to ever leave

you are more than everything

I could ever need

I believe in fairytale things

more than dreams

because everything about you is written

in stories I've read before

you touch my core

make me want more

heal all that's sore

open doors I swore closed long ago

You may never know just what this means

but I cling to you harder

than anything I've ever had

and the best part about it is

you cling back

you make up for what I lack

put up with the way I sometimes act

and that's not always easy

You Need Me

and you've made that clear

you want this to last for years

you wipe my tears

before they fall from my face

you put me in my place

when Im ready to throw the towel in

you tell me I can't fail

because we are destined to win

So the question is where do I begin

when no end is in sight

what do I do

when there's someone worth the fight

when she becomes every part

of the poems I recite

When she is my reason

to smile each night

When everything feels right

what do I do

to really express my love for you

when words don't equate

what does it take

to say what my heart often feels

what makes the final seal

to seal such a deal that's heaven sent

this is it

this is all I need

no longer am I afraid

nor am I a slave to pain

you changed that

you gave me hope back

and I hope that I've done the same

So many times I've loved in vain

proclaimed its name before knowing it

Thought it was love

before others had a chance of showing it

it if wasn't there

I was confident in growing it

and each time I let myself down

planted seeds on unfertile ground

so each time

they died faster than before

did it a few times more

but the same result came

I was ashamed

can't explain how many times

I prayed for rain

but I only saw drought

Thought I was destined to live without

a barren gardener never to harvest

planted seeds

and tended to my grounds the hardest

Now this is where my heart is

I finally see the fruits of my labor

and it's greater than I expected

You were unexpected

but exceed my expectations

you give me so much elation

everything I have been waiting for

was wrapped inside your heart

you presented it to me

and that was the hard part

and I accepted

tended to what's been neglected

resurrected the rose

that tried to grow in the concrete

our love is concrete

so there's no desire to be discreet

with you

I'm weak with you but that's okay

You've showed me strength

in what you say

no only words,

also in the way you love me

security in the way to touch me

protection in the way you hug me

so I get loss in your arms

No need to be alarmed

I don't see harm

just love

no desire to sleep

when I see everything I've dreamed of

I don't want to miss a thing

Being awake is my dream

I Love You,

Your Future Husband

Day 12

Dear Future Wife:

It's 3:30 in the morning and I'm up. Seems like the void of not having you here gets heavy around this time. I always find myself waking up at this exact time in deep thought of you. I wish I knew the answer to why I miss someone I don't know so much. How I can long for a touch, a kiss, and a presence that I haven't felt. But I do more than ever and it hurts. It hurts because I want to know you. I am eager to know what you had to endure in your search for me. How many tears have you had to cry as a result of us not being together. How many nights you stayed up and prayed to God that he revealed who you were suppose to give your heart to. I can't tell you how many nights I've done this. I've tried to place you in the back of my mind so I wouldn't have to deal with the pain of you not being here but it's impossible. Every day I live for you. In every thing I do my thoughts revolve around you. If you knew the preparation that takes place in knowing that you'll be coming soon. So many don't understand why I'm doing what I'm doing. It's hard to really explain to them. They think I'm crazy but if they only have dreamt the dreams I have then they'd know. I've never felt anything like this before. You have captured my heart before you've even been captured by my eyes. I'm so ready to fall in love with you. I'm ready to spend every moment lost and not worry because I know you'll find me. And when you do I know you'll love me like that's the only thing you'll know how to do. My heart longs for you. I'm ready. ..

I Love You,

Your Future Husband

Day 13

Dear Future Wife

I picture me getting lost in your melody

when you and me make music.

I mean what would be more soothing

than the rhythmic tones of your heart beat and mine.

I recall a time where I didn't trust, love or feel anything for anyone.

And like the rising of the sun

you bring me a new day,

you teach me a new way of love.

Help me to see that love wasn't that fictitious dream

I had dreamed of since I was born.

Scared and torn I know you'd take all that was scorched and scorn,

Tethered and worn by the pain of trying.

You'd breathe life into a heart that's dying

And kiss every wound to stop the crying

So my vision wouldn't be blurred anymore.

Massage the places inside my soul that were sore.

Where pain had been victorious in my life for so long

You'd find a way to even the score.

You'd give more than you had to give,

You treat my broken heart like it was a gift and cherish it.

In your hands I'd find more than just something to hold.

I'll find a place where understanding and unconditional love can go

And grow into something more real than reality.

In your hands I'll learn that there's actually a place

Where security secures me so I never have to worry about it again.

as you show me the real definition of a friend,

You'd listen in when I tell you my fears,

You be my shoulder to cry on throughout the years

Even when you felt certain things weren't worth my tears

you'd still listen

never mention I was making a mistake

you'd just sit and wait as I cried

and each tear that fell you'd dry

In your hands I'd find a plan I could stick to.

Someone I could be into without the issue of having to share

Someone that's willing to take the time out to be there

And treat every second, minute, and hour rare because it's priceless

When this world comes against us someone I can fight with

To overcome this fictitious misconception of what love is

When people look at us I want them to be able to know that love lives

Just by our mere presence I want them to feel the essence of us

Dissect our relationship and study how trust supersedes lust

How time was never rushed, our gratitude for each second

Was appreciated much more than the minute and hour hand

How our laid out plan would be to discover this land

And from the moment we began

You'll be holding my hand and my heart

So no longer will I be afraid to walk into the dark

Our love would create the spark I need to see

You'll be the best part of living for me

I'm ready to give you all of me

There's no love too big or small for me

I look forward to the days of you calling me your husband

That's the greatest gift in the end

once you give me your hand

and we say I do

I'll devote every day of my life

learning everything needed for loving you

Eternally Yours,

Your Future Husband

Day 14

Dear Future Wife

Last night we made love

For the first time

Not as woman and man

But as husband and wife

Everything about it felt right

As the moon provided the only light

We needed to see

This night was meant to be

Way before you and me

ever existed

Way before the mention of our I do's

God chose me and you

To go through

the things we went through

To get here

I felt your tears as we embraced

You hid your face

Buried it in my chest

And whispered it was worth the wait

That no other place

but this place mattered

You were no longer afraid

Of what happens after this

We exchanged a kiss

Felt the exchange of energy

Between our lips

I never knew such bliss

Like this before

You cried for more

As our clothes dropped to the floor

There we stood

Secure

You see we both had been pure

Before this moment

Denied ourselves

of the things we wanted

So the desire was evident

Everything about your body

Was heaven scent

I could smell heaven's scent

All over you

I took my time showing you

My appreciation

Cherished everything I was tasting

Experienced the sweetest sensations

With you

Kissed you like I missed you

Explored you like a gift to a child

I wish you could've seen my smile

Then you'd understand now

How I feel

It felt so real

As I kneeled before you

I kissed more of you

The things others took away

At that very moment I restored in you

As we made love

Each stroke was more intense

Than anything we ever dreamed of

The build up

to that moment left us spent

Tears weren't the only things

That left our bodies drenched

As we continued

I showed you

just how much I've missed you

And you did the same

You've never felt a sweeter pain

And I never knew real rain

Til it happened

We gave each other

the stored up passion

We had been keeping

Just for that day

There was really nothing left to say

As we embraced to we fell asleep

Then I woke up and realized

This was just a dream

Your Future Husband

Letter's To My Future Wife

Day 15

Dear Future Wife:

Been up since 1 this morning thinking about you. Seems like each day around this time it happens. Are you dreaming of me? I have this strong belief that you are. My heart feels it. I can't begin to tell you the joy I feel right now. In my search for you I'm discovering so much about myself that I never knew before. Funny how you're making me better without physically being here. I walk with a new sense of direction, a new purpose, and my outlook on life has completely changed. I sit and recall a time when the thought of this wasn't even possible. It wasn't that I didn't want it. It was simply that I had been through so much that I began to lose hope you would come. But how could I lose hope in something I desired like my body needed air to breathe. I remember many nights I cried for you. Prayed that God would reveal you so the hurt I felt would go away but he didn't. I understand now that I wasn't ready for you. That at that moment I couldn't love you the way you deserved to be loved because I was still learning to love myself again. I didn't realize that from previous relationships I had given all of me and I was empty. I had nothing left. It wasn't until about 8 months ago that I realized just how broken I was. There's a saying that goes " one morning I woke up and I woke up". That's exactly what happened. I realized that I no longer wanted a temporary fix to what seemed to be a permanent problem in my life. I wanted you. I realized that through all my searches for forever you had been in a place of your own waiting for me to figure it out. I get it now.

Everything I've went through has prepared me for this moment. I know what I want and it's never been more clearer. But want I want has no comparison to what you need. So right now at this moment I make this vow to you. I vow to never forget what it took to bring us together. I vow to be more than your husband, I'll be your best friend. I vow to show you each day how lucky I am to have u in my life. I vow to hold your hand like it was the only one I should've been holding my entire life. I vow to pray with you and keep God in our relationship because he blessed me with you. I vow to be a leader as well as a protector. Once given your heart I vow to cherish it, keep it safe, and guard it as much as I do my own. For every weakness I vow to be your strength. I vow to never give up regardless of what comes against us. That day we say I do is going to be the greatest day of my life and every day after I'll treat it as such. I'll be your Boaz and I'll always honor your spirit. You are the reflection of God's love for me. My Ruth, my love, and most importantly my best friend. I Love You...

Your Future Husband

Day 16

Dear Future Wife:

It's Monday, the start of a new work week but for me it's the start of another week without you. I can't sit here and act like everything is ok because it isn't. It seems your absence is beginning to become unbearable. I try to do other things to take my mind off you but how could I. You're my nucleus and everything revolves around you. I see you in all I do on a day to day basis. When I pray I see you holding my hands praying with me. When I cry I see you drying my tears. When I sleep I see you laying right next to me and when I dream I always seem to meet you there. The desire for you is evident in everything I do. For the life of me I can't understand how I hold such deep feelings when I don't know who you'll be. There are those that think I'm crazy. They mock me and make jokes about it. But I'm not ashamed to say I feel the way I feel about having you in my life. That's all I ever wanted since I was able to understand what a real marriage meant. I'm not in love with just being in love. I'm in love with the partnership it represents. I'm in life with the union under God it creates. I'm in love with waking up everyday knowing you'll be there to greet me. I'm in love with building a life with my best friend. I'm in love with sharing in the moments that will take our breath away. But most importantly I'm in love with you. So with that being said I present you with this box. The contents of this box will remain hidden till the day I stand before God and give you everything I have. I believe in speaking things into existence so I'll continue to speak your name til the day you come. I love you....

Waiting For Our Forever

Your Future Husband

Day 17

Dear Soul Mate:

For the past few weeks I have written to a figure that's a representation of you. But today I realize that she's not you. She's not everything I want and need you to be. So today this letter is specifically for you. I finally realize that it wasn't my heart calling out to you... It was my soul....How is it that I can say this? How is it that I can place such a calling on my soul? I'll explain....The dictionary defines that soul as " the immaterial essence, animating principle, or actuating cause of an individual life". The Immaterial Essence stood out to me the most because it means a spiritual, rather than physical thing that resides inside of a person. I need you to understand that this is more than physical for me. It's so easy to fall for what the eyes can see but I'm ready to love you blind. Because in that blindness I have to trust that what we have will be everything I've prayed for. I'm ready to be safe with you. I'm ready to provide safety and security in your life so that you know it's okay to fall in love with me. I want you to be secure enough to jump and know that I'd never allow your feet to ever touch the ground. I'll always be there to catch you. So you'll never know what the ground ever feels like. You'll just continue falling. I want to be your best friend. I want to be the one that you tell every secret you've ever kept to and not have to worry about being judged or seen as imperfect because it's in those imperfections that I'll find you to be perfect. I understand that life has had to mature you in ways you never imagined. That's why I want to take the time to know everything about you. I want to be able to comfort you when you cry, reassure you when you have regrets, hold you when you feel alone, listen when you just need a ear, guide you when you're lost, pray for you as much as I pray for me because I realize that this is so much bigger than us. Most importantly I want to take the time needed to get it right. I'm not here to be a temporary solution for you. I am asking for forever. When we meet I want to be the last person you ever give your number to, the last man you ever have to give your heart to, the last time you ever have to worry about waking up alone, and if you should ever cry I want those tears to be of joy, not pain. More than anything else I want to be the man that God created me to be for you. Understand that none of this works without God so I want to do what it takes to makes sure that he stays that strand that keeps us tied together forever. Nothing is possible without that. I can't tell you how long I've been searching for you. How many nights I stayed up in tears praying to him, asking him to give me clarity to why I felt the way I have all these years. Why those that have come into my life have only been for a reason or a season. I've seen so many around me that were sharing in what was meant for them except me. I realize now at this very moment I wasn't ready for you because I wasn't ready for myself. The entire time I was living in the moments God was preparing me for my lifetime... You are my lifetime!!!! You are the one who is going to be a prayer answered, the fresh breath of air, the sunshine I've never experienced, the one who gives me more than the desires of my heart. That's why at this moment, right here, in front of the world I make this proclamation... I'm Ready to receive you unto me. I'm Ready to cherish each day on this earth with you. I'm Ready to tell the world about you. I'm Ready to fall in love. I'm Ready to be your best friend, man, and husband. I'm Ready to pray with you. I'm Ready to wake up each day thanking God for sending you. I'm Ready to love you like no other has ever loved you. I'm Ready to honor you, I'm Ready to cherish you....What I'm trying to say is.......I'M READY

I Love You,

Your Future Soul Mate

Day 18

Dear Future Wife:

The desire to have your head on my chest as you rest is needed. I want to fall asleep with you in my arms because in that very moment I'll know what dreams really feel like. My heart yearns for you. Sleep well baby. I am but a dream away from being with you.

I Love You

Your Future Husband

Day 19

Dear Future Wife

They say a man who fails to plan is one who plans to fail. I can't tell you how many things I have planned for you. I have mapped out a life for us without a life for us being present. But that's how you make me feel. Daily I speak your name into existence and walk in the faith of knowing that my heart's desires will be given to me as long as I keep speaking your name. These letters have become my confessions of devotion for you. I write them in hopes that one day you'll jump off these pages. I etch a carbon copy of the love I have for you right now. Can you feel it? Do you know how much I love you? I pray you do. I long to express what I confess with every beat my heart takes. You are all I want and next to God you're my everything

I Love You

Your Future Husband

Day 20

Dear Future Wife

I often wonder what it's going to be like to kiss you. How your lips would press against mine and the reaction it would cause. I have envisioned the perfect moment in my mind several times and I think I've planned it out perfectly. I'm very aware that things like this are supposed to happen unexpectedly but with the desire I have I want it to be perfect. Who plans things like this?.... I do. But I'm sure you understand that I've waited quite some time for that very moment to take place so to me it's more than just a kiss. It's a taste of what forever will feel like. To kiss the woman that I plan to spend the rest of my life with. To exchange physical as well as emotional energy through gestures of admiration is all I desire. That's why it has to be right. It's funny as I sit here writing this letter I can't stop smiling. Just the thought of you does so much to me. I can't wait til the day all this makes sense. When my mental image can be a physical image. when I will no longer just be dreaming but I will actually be living my dream. There will be no greater joy for me. I'm know patience is a virtue so I'm waiting patiently baby. I'm ready to take that step forward. I'm ready for us to walk in the purpose God created just for us. Are you ready to meet me halfway. I promise I'll lead you from there.... Forever is only a step away....

Yours Forever

Your Future Husband

Day 21

Dear Future Wife

Today has definitely been a very difficult day for me. I witnessed a gentleman propose to his girlfriend. Now don't get me wrong because what I saw was beautiful and I never understood how something so beautiful could hurt so bad. I saw you and I. Not in the same place but definitely experiencing the same emotions. This man poured out his heart and as he spoke I saw me doing the same. I saw me holding your hand and saying.....

Baby

it seems like I've waited for you forever

No poem could ever express

The storms I've weathered

For days like this

when the weather seems fair

I'm more than lucky to have you here

With me

Do you understand what you mean to me

When I feel like a failure

You believe in me

When I feel unwanted

You express your need for me

You call when you're needing me

Letter's To My Future Wife

To come

You hold me when I want to run

My life was dark

But you brought me back the sun

Before you life was dull

But you provide the fun I desire

You do so much more than inspire

When inspiration seems to fade

You find ways

To help the days pain go away

When everyone else bailed on me

You stayed

When I hurt

You prayed

When I was depleted

You gave

You created ways out of no way

I'm finding the right way to say this

I want to make sure my point isn't missed

I never want to wake up without a kiss

Again

You took my torn heart

and created a mend

Saw a boy

And developed a man

When I couldn't lead you took my hand

So now it's time I return the favor

You made my life great

Let me make yours greater

This can't wait a day later

Now is the time

But even at this moment

the words are hard to find

Even this rhyme won't do

I want to grow old with you

if death should comes for us

I want to be holding you

In my heart I know it's you

I want to wake up and see

So on this one knee

I'm asking you to Marry Me......

Sincerely Yours

Your Future Husband

Day 22

Dear Future Wife

Last night I closed my eyes

And to no surprise

you were there

As we lay and stare

No words were shared

As our thoughts aired

Like our favorite movie

We laid still yet moving

Soothing our hearts from the days stress

clothed

but completely undressed

Mentally

You know where my mental be

thinking to myself

How much you're meant for me

As I held you

Intoxicated by your scent as I smelled you

Who knew what a smell could do

As I pull you closer

Letter's To My Future Wife

to fill the empty space

Softly stroke your face

Taste the sweetest taste

from your lips

Like well rehearsed scripts

We continued to play the parts

Nothing physically given but your heart

No desire to ever depart

From this

To stay in your embrace is the only wish

I've wished for years

Nothing is more important

than having your here

Right now

Your eyes

Your smile

Your lips

Your mind

Meet mine

And in the moment we escape time

Together

What's better than this moment

Our soul express everything wanted

Departing is the only opponent we face

In the end

It hurts I have to leave you again

I can't pretend like I'm ok

My thoughts revert back to you

throughout my day

I found the perfect place to stay

Where everything feels ok

Where my pain is taken away

By you

So goodbye won't do

This desire for you is deep

But I guess it'll have to wait

Till I once again fall asleep

Day 23

Dear Future Wife

I love you and I need you here...This is the hardest thing I've hard to endure.

Missing You

Your Future Husband

Day 24

Dear Future Wife

My days seem to merge with each other these days. Can't really find an end to help me understand all this. I know I'm supposed to be tough. I'm supposed to be unfazed but to be totally honest with you..... it hurts like hell. I'm not okay in any way at this moment. My heart yearns for you. I have been speaking your name for quite some time in prayer. I've been asking God to reveal you to me and for a reason I'll never understand..... He Won't. Doesn't he understand how I long for you? How I lay alone at night with constant thoughts of you running through my mind. How I dream of you even when I'm trying to escape the thought of you for a little while. How nothing makes since anymore. How I've lost the desire to consider the "what ifs" because I'm so certain that this will work. All my faith is in you. At times I find myself so frustrated because I have so much that I want to share with you. So much that I want to show you and it feels like time lost is the only thing I have obtained. None of this makes sense to me right now. I look at some who have that love to call their own. I see their happiness and every part of my being wants that. There's something about the look of a man in love that speaks more words that his lips could ever speak. I want to share that language with you. I want us to be so in sync with each other that our spirit can connect on every level so words never have to be spoken when it comes to the desires of our heart. I'm sure you know how it feels waking up each day and not having me there. That empty feeling that sits inside your heart. That sensation that never seems to be fulfilled. That joy that you can't find when everything around you seems to be going right. Those tears that you have to keep bottled up when you see someone else having what you know you were created to have.Yes.... that feeling!!!! I swear as I'm typing this letter I feel it. My soul calls out for you right now. The need for you is severe. Most will never understand me. I can't begin to tell you the ridicule I receive daily from writing you. People don't understand how I can write to a woman I have never met or seen. What's crazy is people walk this earth every day breathing oxygen they can't see but they believe they are breathing. What's wrong with believing in something as beautiful as having someone to complete me? I will admit that at times they knock me off my course but I remind myself that you are out there waiting for me. That this is so much bigger than anyone will ever understand. I know what I want. I've never been so sure of anything else in my life. So from this moment on every day i'll speak your name into existence til that day you come and even after it will be the only name I'll ever speak....

I Love You
Your Future Husband

Day 25

Dear Future Wife

It's crazy how everything around me gives me inspiration to write to you. There is so much to be inspired about right now. Because of you and the feelings that I have for you God is making provisions in my life in preparation for your arrival. You have no idea of the eagerness that I hold in my heart right now. I'm like a kid in the candy store that just found his favorite candy. I can't wait to get you and unwrap all the goodness you posses. That will be one of the most amazing moments in my life. I swear it feels like I have waited an entire lifetime for you. But in waiting I can say this one thing.... It will all be worth it when you come... I pray that you are in perfect health and you know that I love you with all I have inside me

Yours Forever,
Your Future Husbad

Day 26

Dear Future Wife:
Have you ever thought about the way we will meet each other. I am sitting hear losing my mind right now. Will I recognize you? Will our attraction be instant or will it develop over time? Who will make the first move? What do your hugs feel like? What will our conversation be like? What will happen on our first date and when we kiss what will that first kiss say? We both know that the first kiss says so much. Why am I sitting hear thinking about this? There are a thousand other things I should be doing but I can't get these thoughts out my head. You have no idea the plans that I am making for us. The places that we have never visited that we will visit. The foods we've never tired that we will try. Everything about what we experience will be new and exciting and it will be tailor made to fit us. I look forward to sharing life with the woman that will be my best friend. I hope that you are getting prepared for what's about to take place. Well it's time for me to get back to my day dream. Love you so much

Forever Yours
Your Future Husband

Day 27

Dear Future Wife

I can't sleep tonight baby. I have tossed and turned most of the night and I just can't seem to get comfortable. This bed just doesn't feel the same anymore. It's crazy because nothing about it has changed except the fact that you are not in it. Since I began searching for you nothing is the same anymore. I find it hard at times to go certain places because I see the image of you in so many faces but I don't want to confuse them with you. I want to be certain it's you when you come. I no longer desire the false representations of you. They don't add up to the woman that God has already created you to be for me. I know that day you stand in front of me God will provide me with the feeling that I prayed for since I learned what real love really was. Til then I'll continue to take comfort in these letters til you can hear me say everything I feel for you. I pray that you are sleeping well my love.

With My Deepest Love,
Your Future Husband

Day 28

Dear Future Wife

This morning I needed to write

Had to find a way to get my thoughts right

About you

Spent another night without u

But I don't doubt you did the same

I found another way to say your name

Wife seems plain

So let me explain

I see you as the healer of my pain

The one that keeps me sane

The constant thought on my brain

That won't leave

The one who knows what I need

The one that believes in me

Sees things in me I never did

Who brings joy to this life I live

Daily

The only one who could save me

From myself

The only one who could help

The restorer of my health

My only source of wealth

When I feel depleted

The one who'll fight for me

When I feel defeated

It's you who sees me.

Before the world could see me

As a man

When I'm confused

you help me understand

That things in life

don't always go according to plan

But plans do work

When you recognize the worth

In them

Put forth the effort

And start working them diligently

I wish you knew

what you're healing in me

With each letter

Wish you knew

How you make my life better

As I prepare for you

Letter's To My Future Wife

Go in prayer for you
Vow to be there for you
So when we say I do
We can start our journey to forever
Knowing that nothing can destroy
What God put together
In us
In you I place all my trust
I vow to be patient
When there's the desire to rush
with you
If I'm going to be tied to anything
I'd rather be stuck to you
Your For Eternity
Your Future Husband

Day 29
Dear Future Wife
Your Hands
I never knew how delicate they were
Til you held me
And when you held me
You did more than feel me
You filled me
Got past the walls of protection
To reveal the real me
I had closed off
You uncovered what was loss
Gave me back all I lost
In love
Help me think of things
I couldn't think of
Or maybe didn't want to
There's nothing you won't do
For me
You're for me
You place no other before me
This was destined before we
Were thought of
Who thought love
Would be found now
But I don't question how it came
I've spelled your name
On several pages
Professed our love on countless stages
Filled the empty spaces
With thoughts of you

Letter's To My Future Wife

If you could've seen the places
I sought for you
The emotional battles
I've fought from you
Not being here
The stories told through my tears
So many years wasted
So many different faces
But I had to face it
They weren't meant
for permanent placement in my life
That spot is only meant for my wife
The one that'll provide light
To my darkest parts
The one who'll give me her heart
Without me asking
Make up the things I'm lacking
The one who causes
the greatest reaction
For me
I finally see
Its you I've been waiting for
Praying for
Day and night
I'm ready to invite you in my life
Make sure this time
we both get it right
So the world can see
You're the only girl for me
Sincerely
Your Future Husband

Day 30
Dear Future Wife

Right not none of this feels fair. I'm tired of laying without you. I can't sleep from thoughts of you running through my mind. Is it supposed to feel life this. Why do I have to hurt from something I desire so much. I know patience is a virtue and the best things in life are worth waiting for. It's just really hard right now. I get off work and come home to an empty house when I'd rather be coming home to you. It's not the easiest reality to face. I long for the day that all this makes sense.

I love you

Your Future Husband

Day 31
Dear Future Wife

How can one wake up heavy hearted from the thought of you.
These past few days that's what I've been dealing with. Seems these
days there are so many who pose as you. They present all the
qualities I look for but when it comes time to show action they fall
short. I don't think they understand the sincerity behind the words
I speak. This isn't some show. This isn't a dream I'm trying to sell.
I'd rather live one with you. But I'm starting to believe that's
impossible. But how is that even possible. How can a man who
speaks on love daily be without it? How can I have all the qualities
of a good man but lack the one to share it with. I swear none of this
makes sense anymore. This feeling of emptiness is becoming
unbearable these days. I try to fill it with the faith that one day it'll
all come together. But I need something. A reminder, a glimpse, a
sign that I'm not in this alone... I don't feel your presence anymore.
Those things that gave me hope seem so distant right now. I pray
this is only temporary. I'm trying to be strong but I'm beginning to
weaken. Please come to me. I love you

Your Future Husband

Day 32
Dear Future Wife

Today the thought of our family came across my mind. You have no idea what that thought is doing. To share life with the woman I get to spend the rest of my life with. That's one of the greatest gifts I could ever receive. I can't wait for the day you run up to me with this huge smile on your face telling me you're pregnant. I am almost sure I'll cry but it will be a good one... You don't understand what that would mean to me. You don't know what I've endured to get to a moment like that in my life. I would kiss your belly everyday. I would jump to the midnight runs to the store because you're craving a baked potatoes with sour cream and chives or ice cream and pickles. Whatever you desired I'd travel stores to find it for you. Then when I got back home I'd rub your feet while you feed our child all those strange combinations. I would lay there every night talking to your belly telling our child how much I love him/her and how I can't wait til they were here. And when we slept the only way to be comfortable is holding you and your belly so I can feel our child move around. Swear we'd take some of the most beautiful pictures capturing those precious moments. Then the day our child comes I'll be right there by your side through everything. We'd breath together, pray together, scream together, push together, and when I child comes we'd thank God together. You guys will be my everything. I swear that day is going to be one of my greatest accomplishments... I love you so much....

Your Future Husband

Day 33
Dear Future Wife

It's moments like this that everything make sense. Why I cry, why I hurt, why despite the ridicule I face daily I never waiver. I'm not in love with being in love. I'm in love with the possibility of a love I've never experienced before. So many will never experience this feeling. So many will walk this earth and just exist. But that's not me. I don't just want to exist. I want to live life to the fullest. When people say I'm dreaming I want to be able to proudly say "no I'm living a dream" that will be because I'll have everything I have ever dreamed of. I'll finally know completion because I'll finally know you. Do you have any idea how much I pray for you? I know you're being molded just the way I prayed to God. In prayer I always ask him to bless me with the woman I'll love and spend my life with til the last breath I take be in telling you how much I love you and even in death our love lives til you join me. I prayed that everything we experience be the closest thing to heaven for the both us..... I finally get it. I'm finally starting to understand why you aren't here yet. God has to finish preparing us for that forever. Have you dreamt of me? Have you pictured you and I together. I wish u could see the dreams i have. You would rest assured in the images you'd see. We've got a forever standing in front of us. All we have to do is walk into it. I can't wait til the day you take my hand and we begin walking together.

Forever Is Only A Step Away

Your Future Husband

Day 34
Dear Future Wife

Do you believe in love at first sight? That it's possible in one encounter you could fall in love with a person. I do! I definitely believe it's very possible and to be honest I think that's how you and I will meet. I never realized until today how important a conversation is. A very wise woman told me "It's in that conversation, those first five sentences that you make a decision if that person interest you enough to continue the conversation and go further." I sit and picture our first conversation and can't help but smile. Crazy thing is I know exactly what I'll say to you. Do you understand how I long for that conversation? For the chance to tell you that our meeting was planned and prayed for way before our eyes ever had the chance to meet. I get excited just thinking about it. I know we'll get lost in the conversation just like we'll get lost in each other. But the benefit of being lost this time will be that I know only you can find me. I'm ready to be found. I'm ready to find you. I can't wait till all this make sense. I have this bottled up emotion that belongs to you. All I'm waiting on you to do is twist off the cap and watch it flow endlessly. Loving you is going to be one of the best things I ever do. I love you

Your Future Husband

Day 35
Dear Future Wife

For the first time in a long time I don't feel alone. That empty space is no longer there. Funny thing about prayer is when you have faith you usually get an answer. I can't begin to tell you how much I've prayed for you. How despite minor set backs I never lost hope. I kept believing in you. Do you understand how strong my faith is? If I sat here and told you everything I've been through you'd wonder how I'm still trying. I know the power of love. I know what it produces merely by what you've produced in me. Just the sound of your voice can break any stronghold that held me. I look forward to many conversations that will get lost in. I look forward to waking up and feeling as I do now.... Complete! Do you understand that you already complete me? That the power you hold inside of you gives me all I need to continue down this journey because I know that you'll be right there with me. That's what makes this so worthwhile. A forever with the woman of my dreams. But the best part about it is I won't have to dream it anymore. I'll be experiencing it. You have no idea what's in store for you.... For us..... For our family. I'm preparing for the best part of life.... Baby I'm preparing for you.

I Love You

Your Future Husband

Day 36

Dear Future Wife

Today my thoughts run free with you. Seems like my nights and dreams only hold room for you. Do you understand the power of prayer? The amazing thing about it is if you have faith the size of a mustard seed you can have everything your heart desires. There was so many times I was ready to throw the towel in. So many days I wasn't sure if u existed. I put so many things in the place that was created for you to occupy that space so I wouldn't hurt anymore from not having you. But I realize nothing can ever replace you. You are completion for me. But more than that you are the Gift God has stored up for me. It brings me so much joy knowing that God took time out of his busy schedule to create you just for me and me for you. I understand why none of the others before you made it. They were reasons and seasons. I had to learn who I was and what I desired in a wife but no one but you is meant to be my lifetime. The woman who will stand next to me and confess her undying love for me. The one I can be vulnerable with and know that she'll guard and treat it is as something sacred. She'll protect me as much as I protect her. No one else can do that but you. I know that now more than ever before. I wake up feeling complete merely from the thought of you. I know our story is about to be written for the world to see. When people ask me who you are I can proudly say I'm her favorite line and she's my signature but together we make poetry. Forever doesn't seem that far away anymore. Heaven on earth is only a step away. God has prepared my Angel, my Ruth, my Good Thing and I make this confession.... I stand here in wait of the day you take my hand and we become one. I thank God in advance for you. He heard my prayers and cries daily and sent comfort to soothe every hurt. To the world you are my helpmate but to me you are balance. The woman that makes everything right. The one who makes up for all I lack. The one that gives back everything that was taken from me. I'll give my last breath making you happy and in that last breath you'll know this..... I Love You

Yours Now and Forever

Your Future Husband

Day 37

Dear Future Wife

If I never knew before this moment....... Everything before you makes this moment so worth it.... I think that I have found you. I feel that my search is over but only God can be sure. I'm about to go into prayer right now to get a better understanding of just what this is. But whatever it is I am enjoying this feeling.

Your Future Husband

Day 38

Dear Future Wife:

We had intimacy

Way before we were intimate

You studied intricate parts of me

Just to be a part of me

Now my heart can see

What was once hard to see

Before you came

Way before the mention of your name

It Seemed pain had a hold on me

Lovers were scolding me

For not being

what I was supposed to be

In their eyes

They ignored cries

But you heard them

Everything I'm ready to give

You deserve it

You've been observing for a short time

And still managed to find the line

Connected to my heart

Hooked it up to yours

And gave me a start

Repaired the parts that were scarred

Performed countless operations

In the dark

Just to make sure my parts run

Smoothly

When I hurt you'd soothe me

As much as I wanted you

You pursued me

You saw right through me

So we had a natural connection

From the start we were connected

No one in the room but us

Countless hours of conversation

To remove the lust

Patience is a virtue

So we refuse to rush

But loving you comes naturally

Determined to make sure

No man comes after me

So it has to be right

I want love past life

A union under Christ

Letter's To My Future Wife

I'm talking Husband and Wife with you

On your darkest days

I'll be the light for you

If practice makes perfect

Then I'll get it right for you

Where others hesitated

I'll go right for you

When you feel defeated

I step in and fight for you

Life ain't living

If it ain't life with you

That's why I stay up all night

And write to you

You're so much more than affirmation

You're heaven's confirmation

The one God designated

to be mine forever

There's really no other way

To end this letter

You've made my life better

Than the way it began

I Love You So Much

Your Future Husband And Your Best Friend

Day 39

Dear Future Wife

They say in the quiet moments in your life your heart speaks loudly. Well this is one occasion I can say it's yelling. Someone i know once told me to write my vision and make it plain. For as long as I can recall that's what I've been doing in regards to you. But to be honest I never expected that vision to take shape the way it's beginning to. My heart is opening to the anticipation of you. Oh how I look forward that day. Everything about these moments make perfect sense. I'm so in love with you. Everything about you gives me hope for things to come between us. But I fear the world won't understand the Love we share. They will be quick to judge. But how could they. How could they ever understand the power of prayer if they've never prayed for you. If they've never fasted to have clarity in the plan that God created for them. These are the things that I endured to have a forever with you. Forever.... That's a word that most will never understand but I desire that with you. I want that feeling that comes from waking up to you everyday. Spending countless hours getting lost in you. Learning the things that make you who you are so I can be the balance to your scale. I want hours of you in my arms. I want you to feel how my heart skips beats when you kiss me and in those kisses I'll know what the next 70 years of my life will feel like. I want to sing to you. Even though I can't sing I look forward to the smile you'll give as I sing it. I look forward to those nights we can just lay in bed and reflect on our day. And when we make love I want our passion to be expressed in countless physical actions. I want to experience a glimpse of heaven every time we make love. More than anything else I want us to grow old together raising our children and displaying unconditional love as the example for them to follow. I look forward to each day with you. Most importantly I look forward to telling you that I love you every chance I get.

I love you baby

Your Future Husband

Day 40

Dear Future Wife

Funny but lately all my conversations have been of you. Can't tell you how good it feels to have something positive to speak of. I sit and recall several days like today where nothing about it was positive. Despite being around family and friends there was always a void I dealt with. After several years of not knowing what it was I finally understand. I have been lost without you. I filled that void with so many of the wrong things and when it was all said and done I was still empty. I long for the holidays now. I want to be able to wake up to you and our family and celebrate in the moments we will share. I sit and think about how that's going to feel. Finally the completion I have been looking for my entire life. Today is thanksgiving and I can sit and picture is waking up, cooking breakfast, and preparing dinner for the night. Pulling out the Christmas stuff so we can get prepared for the next holiday. I am eager to know what it feels like to do this with you. Our first holidays, our first memories, our first everything together. I long for that more than you can ever understand. Its been lonely without you. But I know this is only temporary. You'll be here soon to make this feeling disappear. I pray that you are enjoying your holiday and I hope you are thinking of me.

Yours Forever

Your Future Husband

Day 41

Dear Future Wife

You know for the longest time I've searched for why I am the way I am. Why when I love a person I love with every fiber in my being. Why when I watch movies on the happiest moments of the movie my heart beats faster. Why when it rains the only thing I can think of is being with the woman I love. I walked this earth for 30 years hopelessly in love with the image of the woman God designed just for me. Despite being hurt many occasions I never gave up believing that you would come. I prayed for you to the point my knees were numb and just when I felt weary God gave me a sign that he heard every prayer. That loneliness has subsided, that doubt is nonexistent, and for the first time in my life I'm loving boastfully. I walk with a new walk, with my chest high and confess my undying devotion to you. For you I love out loud. For you I love like that's the only thing I was created to do. I love with no fear, with no reservation. What I feel for you is unconditional. I don't fear anything coming against us because of my prayers. Your timing couldn't have been more perfect. I'm glad you're here now. I feel like that Forever I have dreamed of is finally coming and I couldn't be more happy. So to whom it may concern.... You are no longer a thought for me. You are the rising of the sun on my darkest days. My place of refuge when I'm in pain. Because of you I smile again. So thank you and I love you more than you'll ever understand.

Forever Grateful,

Your Future Husband

Day 42

Dear Future Wife

This letter is different in so many ways. There is so much I need to
say to you. So many thoughts that run through my mind at this
time. Before you the thought of Forever seemed so far-fetched.
Seemed like only a dream I dreamt and many didn't understand
that. How could a man love a the thought of a woman he hadn't
met yet? They never really knew just how tangible the thought of
you was. I may not have physically seen you but I'd dream you on
many occasions. Your touch, your scent, the way I'd feel as you
walked in the room to greet me, the way you'd touch my face as
we'd embrace. I knew you before I knew. Everything about
moments like this makes this more than confirmation for me. It's
an affirmation that dreams can come true. I'm happy to say I don't
have to dream anymore. Seems that those prayers I prayed for God
to reveal you have been answered. I've smelled that scent, felt that
touch, and know what each greeting feels like. Basically what I'm
trying to say is you're no longer a thought for me. You're a dream
projected into reality for my eyes to see daily. Our story is being
written in front of the world and I'm loving everything I'm reading.
But I understand there's so much more to this story that time has
to develop so I read slowly. Carefully dissecting each line to get the
full understanding of what we already share. But if you don't mind
I want to give my side of the story to you. Everything about our
timing was destined. I met you when my soul was ready to love
again and there you stood. In a room full of people but it was just
me and you there. I couldn't help but stare when I first saw you.
Then I lost you but only for a second. Your attention was
misdirected but never directed away from me. Where you in the

same place as me? As we stood in a place where we could converse. You knew I was well versed but no lines were rehearsed at that moment. Fear was the only opponent I'd face as I figured out a way to occupy your space for a second of time. Can't explain how the words were hard to find. But you assured me I was fine as I release thoughts on my mind to you. I lost track of time with you. Felt the chills down my spine with you and at that moment I knew it was real. Every prayer revealed. Every want fulfilled that first moment I laid eyes on you. I was surprised you noticed me. Felt like I was holding a sign so you could know it's me and you did. Now we step forward in this life we'll live together. The best is yet to come but all I see is Forever.

Yours Always

Your Future Husband

Day 43

I have always been a lover of the romance language. There is something about it that makes it so amazing to me. Maybe it's the fact that is involves romance. I studied this language for a few years and I wanted to take this time to say....

chère épouse avenir

Je voulais profiter de cette occasion pour vous dire combien Je te aime. merci d'être le seul à prendre mon souffle. Je te aime

votre futur mari

Day 44

It's 43 days in and the one thing that has not changed is my love and devotion towards a life with you. I sit in amazement and what God is laying before me right now. He is taking the time to build this bond that will be one to last for the rest of my life. He is creating a perfect work. The crazy thing about time is not being able to control it. I sit and wonder if I could control time would I have wanted to fast forward to these moments right now. To be totally honest with you I wouldn't want to . I love the man that I am becoming. I love the work that God is doing on me in preparation of you. The areas that were weak he is producing strength and the areas that are not meant for me he is breaking the strongholds that were placed on me. All this is being done on his time. I am truly blessed right now because he is giving me a sign that the best is yet to come. I can't wait to share that best with you.

Your Future Husband

Day 45

Today started of like any other normal day except that feeling of loneliness is completely gone. It's the most freeing feeling I could feel at this moment. I don't wake up in tears. I don't wake up feeling empty. I wake up with a renewed mindset and outlook on the days ahead. God wouldn't have brought me this far if it weren't for a far greater reason than my mind could ever comprehend. I feel one step closer to you. I feel that day is almost hear. I feel......
That's it I can finally feel again.....

I Love You

Your Future Husband

Day 46

Dear Future Wife

I dreamt of you last night. How is it that you can occupy my mind in the moments where I am supposed to be sound asleep allowing my body the time to rest up for the activities of the day. My dreams have become so vivid. Like watching a movie on television and smiling because one of the scenes touched your heart. That's how I feel daily. I wake up refreshed from those dreams. Is this God's way of telling me to just be patient a little while longer? Are you dreaming of me in those moments where my mind only holds you? I am trying to make out what this is but I can't. All that I can say is a look forward to the moment when my head touches my pillow each night because in that moment I find you.

See You Soon,

Your Future Husband

Day 47

What will you look like? What physical feature will help me to know that it's you. I have dreamt of you so many nights but I have yet to see your face. But I feel your touch, hear your voice, see the way you walk, and know how hard my heart beats whenever you are around. How can dreams feel so real? I've touched you on so many occasions, danced with you, sung to you, laughed with you, cried with you, but I have yet to know how angelic your face is. I ask God why won't he reveal you to me. I cry out to him because at times I don't feel it's fair that I can't see who you are. I'm ready to love you. I'm ready for the answers to be revealed... God I'm ready!!!

Your Future Husband

Day 48

Dear Future Wife

Lately my thoughts have been everywhere. In this search for you I have found out so much about me. The things that I once believed were important now hold no value in my life. Because of you I found love, I found faith, I found patience, I found trust, I found peace, but more than anything else I found me. I can't begin to tell you how lost I was. In my search for you I lost myself in false representations of you. I really didn't know who I was anymore. I wasn't living. I was just existing in a world where I felt invisible. I can't begin to tell you how good it feels to see a reflection I recognize again. I thank you for being that guiding light in my darkest of days. I finally see what my purpose is. I know longer fear walking in that purpose because I'm very aware that you will be walking with me. That's the most comforting feeling to feel. I'm so ready to love out loud when it comes to you. Unlimited gestures of affection, countless hours of expressing just what I've been missing my whole life. I look forward to that. Till then I'll count the hours till.

I love you,

Your Future Husband

Day 49

Dear Future Wife

We share more than just computer keys

When she be provoking me

On rainy days I think of the ways

She could be stroking me

Mentally

She knows where my mental be

She's meant for me

So we get lost in conversation

Can't explain the elation I feel

But it's real

Guess only time reveals

Our destination

So I get lost in situations

We share

Seems rare

But it's there

Just enough for me to feel

She's here for me

Even if she can't be near me

She hears me

Wants, desires, and wishes

She let's me vent while she listens

Let's me in with resistance

She's been hurt before

Couldn't see her hurting more

From my hands

Desire to be different than other man

She's had

Carefully showing her what I have

To give

The way I live

And love

Hoping to be that knight

She speaks of

She speaks love

In action

Her hugs create a reaction

I react to when I see her

Don't want to seem needy

But at times I feel I need her

My thoughts lately be her

I dream her

Daily

That smile she gives

Whenever she be waving

The tone of her voice

From everything she's saying

That's why I'm waiting

For the right time

Catch her in her right mind

Just to let her know

These are more than some nice lines

I offer

How I want to rub her down

Till her skin feels softer

Knowing what she needs

When her speech begins to falter

I'll go silent

And my touch will be all I'm providing

But we're far from things like this

Damn she makes me dream like this

See things like this

when she message me

Letter's To My Future Wife

I'll get lost in the keys

And forget I'm me

Dreams of we

Even if that never existed

She leaves me wishing

For this to be our reality

Never felt the fallacy

With her

Went through hell just to get her

She creates lasting memories

So I can never forget her

She's a permanent fixture

In my life

Deemed wife

Before rings and invites

We thought of

Sought love but she found me

When my emotions are in the air

She grounds me

When I feel alone

she surrounds me

She never hesitates to be around me

She's my own personal savior

Letter's To My Future Wife

That's why every moment we share

I savor

She made me better

Now it's my turn to return the favor

make her life greater

give her all I've got

and still same some for later

it's true

I'm living the best parts of life

because of you

Your Future Husband

Day 50

Dear Future Wife

Today is a realization that I won't always be superman. Today I'm just Clark Kent. My thoughts are everywhere, my emotions are up in the air, and I can't make sense of anything right now. These are the times that I'll need you most. Your understanding, your thoughtfulness, your compassion, your comfort, but most importantly I need your Love. Days like this will be the most trying times for the both of us but these are the time your cape will come out. I need your strength. I need your smile. I need your reassurance that everything will be ok. I need your arms open, ready to receive, revive, reaffirm my faith. This world takes so much from me as a man. So today I need you. My Lois Lane, My Superwoman.

Sincerely

Your Future Husband

Day 51

Dear Future Wife

They say call things be not as though they were and for months I have spoke you into existence. Despite the ridicule I faced I never gave up my search for the one that would complete me. I wrote your name on several pages and I'm proud to say everything is coming together. They say behind every good man is an amazing woman. Well this book is dedicated to that amazing woman. The one who helped me think outside the box. The one who inspired me to be better than my circumstance. The one who healed this broken man. The one who answers my prayers daily. The one who saved me. This is dedicated to My Future Wife.... It's time and the timing couldn't have been more perfect.

Yours Forever

Your Future Husband

Day 52

Dear Future Wife

I want that

my friends think I'm crazy kinda Love

That no if, ands, but, or maybe kinda love

That daily you come and save me kinda love

That everything about you is elating kinda love

That in hard times I'm staying kinda love

That open my heart

so you can see what you gave me kinda Love

I want that real kinda Love

No afraid to tell you how I feel kinda Love

That what the world broke you heal kinda love

That wake up early

and cook you a full course meal kinda Love

That Vivian and Uncle Phil kinda love

That protected kinda love

The parts that died

but you resurrected kinda Love

That giddy when you call me kinda Love

That give you all of me kinda love

There's nothing to big or small kinda love

That you're my destiny kinda love

Despite what the world takes

You get the best of me kinda Love

That we create the perfect recipe kinda love

That daily you're impressing me kinda Love

That reap from what you invest in me

kinda Love

That when you touch me I get weak kinda love

That everything about you is sweet kinda Love

That watch you while you sleep kinda love

That when you kiss me my heart skips a beat

Kinda love

That sweep you off your feet kinda Love

I simply just want that Kinda Love.....

Sincerely,

Your Future Husband

Day 53

Dear Messenger of Love

I want to know

what's it's like to get lost with you.

Wait for the rescue party

to come through

just so we can find each other.

I want to be more than your lover.

Past the acts permitted under covers.

I want to learn the stitching

that keeps you together.

I commend you.

I've seen the things

you've been through.

Giving freely of yourself

without someone to defend you.

You say you're broken....

Well let me mend you.

When it comes to loving you

I want to do more than pretend to.

I want to study the essence that is you.

That way you'd never fall short

in anything.

I want to be your living dream

when things seem to be a nightmare. Make things right

when life just don't seem fair.

Provide that reassurance

when you feel scared.

Provide that surplus

when love seems scarce.

I just want to be there,

right by your side.

Allow my heart to speak freely

when the words

are hard to find with you.

I want to take the time with you.

Go through the process

just so our progress can be blessed. This is one test I've never
studied for

but I'm sure I'll get a perfect score.

Be the man that you adore

from now until forever.

Dear messenger of love

there's nothing better..... Than you

Sincerely Yours

Your Future Husband

Day 54

Dear Future Wife

I never wanted to count the seconds before today. But it seems like since you came my way those seconds mean so much more than they ever did. In those seconds I live more than I've ever lived. I've experienced a love that's heaven sent. I no longer ask God where heaven is and I owe it all to you. Those prayers I prayed for years were calls for you and you finally responded. You took a man that was once broken hearted, removed that guards that guarded and managed in a short time to love me the hardest. So let me tell you where my heart is because of you. I'm in love with you but I'm past the physical. Daily I journey your mental just to be connected to your spiritual. The mold created for my wife was meant for you. So I'm praying I get to do all these things....

1. Daily I'd tell confess you're the woman of my dreams.

2. We'll always be a team

3. In passionate moments will be the only time you raise your voice to ever scream

4. I'll strive to give you everything

5. Treat you like a queen

6. You'll never want for anything if it's up to me

7. Daily I'll set your heart free

8. I'll give you all of me

9. Be excited when you're calling me

10. Have you constantly fall for me

11. Your insecurities will never be small to me

12. Display a love for all to see.

13. Be all you ever need and desire

14. Be the one who inspires you

15. Work enough to retire you

16. Let you do all you aspire to

17. Watch you elevate to the higher you

18. Light a fire in you that can never be put out

19. Nothing but encouragement comes from my mouth

20. Be your assurance when you have doubt

21. Be the surplus when you experience drought

22. Back up what I write about

23. Create new dates and take you out constantly

24. Hold you when fears says run from me

25. Bask in the sun with me

26. Await a beautiful daughter or son with me

27. Make sure you always know you're the one for me.

28. After its all said and done you'll see

29. You're more than the world you're the sun for me

In 30 seconds look at what you've done for me.

I Love You,

Your Future Husband

Day 55

Dear Future Wife

What will we do when problems arise? How will be able to overcome them. I pray that we can be a unit united with one common goal and that's to always stay together. I know that at times I will upset you. I know that I won't always be able to deliver on what I want to do for you. Unforeseen things can happen but the question I am left to ask is how to overcome them where we both come out happy. I am so big on trying to get it right because for so long I have gotten it wrong. I want this to work. I want this to last an eternity. I pray that you feel the same way. I love you

Your Future Husband

Day 56

Dear Future

The weather is changing and with the change of weather comes the change in season. But not in the physical sense of the word. I mean in every aspect of my life I see change happening. I see ties I once had being broken, new alliances created, but more than anything else I see a stronger faith in the fact that you are almost here. I can't begin to tell you the joy I feel in knowing that soon we will be united as one. I am very aware that there's a process and I want to learn whatever it takes to complete that process with you. I am so ready to love you with everything I have in me. I am so ready to be the man you desire, and I am ready to see what God has in store for us.

I Love You

Your Future Husband

Day 57

Dear Future Wife

Today was really difficult for me. I have to be honest with you about something. I have this void that seems to really take a toll on my emotions. It's like I know that God will grant me the desires of my heart but I wish I knew his timing. I desire you so much right now. At times I want to yell to heaven and ask God to speed up the process a little for me. It hurts not having you hear right now to share in all the things that I have going on. I need you to provide me with the encouraging words I need right now because I'm fighting the spirit of giving up. I'm ashamed to even admit that but I have to be honest with you. I don't want to but it gets really hard. I guess I need to pray harder. I'm going to lay down and hopefully I will meet you in that place where we are together.

Your Future Husband

Day 58

Dear Future Wife

I was asked today what I will do once I found you? Would the letters stop? Would I be done? My answer to them was how could I stop writing about a woman that is going to bless my life. How can I not express the love and the joy that I am receiving because of her. I want the world to know of you. I want them to understand that prayer works. That despite the many roadblocks in life if you have faith anything is possible. I want them to share in the joy that I will experience each and every day and celebrate with us. I look forward to writing those letters. I know that the level of love expressed in those letters will be far stronger than anything I put on this paper. I am so excited about the possibilities of you....

Forever

Your Future Husband

Day 59

Dear Future Wife

I wrote about you today. I sit and laugh while saying that because I write about you every day... Hope you like it...

She gave birth to intuition

did I forget to mention

her intentions were pure

She produced cures for my ailments

Now my ailment can heal itself

Found worth in my wealth

put in work for herself

Letter's To My Future Wife

So she deserves the key

tells me daily she deserves me

But she's not ready for commitment

but the acts we're committing

are with intentions for more

she touches my core

swore to keep it sacred

If I resisted she'd take it

careful not to break it

Doesn't try hard it's basic

gave faith to the faithless

so she must be heaven sent

unaware of where the time went

feels like she spent eternity

learning me

So she can't fail

blueprint of my heart etched like braille

so she feels me

Can't give her nothing but the real me

flaws and all

She loves me big or small

feeds my mind, body, and soul

put me above all, she sacrificed

Letter's To My Future Wife

Doesn't need a ring to be deemed wife

on her knees twice daily

she prays for me

more than I do myself

there for me

when I feel there's no one else

She helps

So I never feel alone

creates a home

so I never roam the streets

Anoints my head

then bows to my feet

She calls me king

More than I could ever dream

So I stay awake

not to miss anything

What we share is deemed necessary

It's scary

I'm loving hard already

Hearts heavy

from what she gives

can't get with the life she lives

but dying to live with her by my side

Letter's To My Future Wife

We ride

putting our pride aside to enjoy it

more enjoyment

without knowing the destination

more elation in situations

she keeps me elevated

pass the physical

but damn the physical is appealing

reeling toward the feeling of the way she feels

natural

everything is real

so I kneel often

but her skin softens my rest

Found rest in her chest

pass her breast

I told y'all its pure

No sexual contact needed

that would make our love impure

obscure our vision

from the things God envisioned for us

lust turns gold to rust

I hold the Midas touch

So I'm careful with my hands

cautiously

carrying out the plan

that God intended

broken hearts need rebuilding

and I'm building a better world for us

just trust what I touched is Golden

It's your heart I'm holding

molding a queen

to rule on the side of her king.

Your Future Husband

Day 60

Dear Future Wife

Never thought it would come to this,
but I guess the inevitable I had to face.
Never known how one woman could occupy so much space.
This is a feeling that I feel in my bones.
It's safe to say that I got "A Love Jones"
See you completes in ways I way i seem to hold no control.
So it's only right that I allow you a piece of my soul
Because the heart doesn't equate the sum of what it takes
To label you my soul-mate.
So it must be fate that I have to wait for the chance
To dance that dance of romance to a song never ending.
But in order to get there it has to be a beginning
And I chose to listen to what love says.

You're good nutrients so each day I stay fed
Off the love you give.
Never had to look for the definition of what love is
Because daily you show me.
I and life are forever changing but you know me.
Never met someone that was able to grow me
Like sun to the trees do,
for me you are the wind so in the end
I do what the leaves do and blow in many directions.
You're my life's lesson
And I am ready to learn all that I need to be educated.
There's nothing that needs to be contemplated,
I know I'm in the right place,
at the right time,
receiving the right information.
What we share is the thing that builds nations.
So never do I have to feel alone.
It's safe to say that I have " A Love Jones"
But these are not "blues for Nina"
These are simply cause I need you.
I'm ready to receive you unto me.
Everything about you sets me free
So whenever I lock down
you get the key to open all doors
Picks me up when I fall on all four,
massages every muscle
so I'm not at all sore,
fulfills every need so there's no need for more
To my life's story you're the perfect ending.

We were destined in genesis
So you become my beginning,
never failed at anything,
Because you're my definition of winning.
So whenever I feel like sinning
You refine my spirit.
Because of you I am a true man
So now I want for the day we stand hand in hand
And vow to love for all eternity
God, You, The Kids, and Me
I love you
Your Future Husband to be

Day 61

Dear Future Wife

As the holiday approaches I wonder what's in store for me. I have always walked this earth feeling empty around this time. There was always something missing. I couldn't quite figure out what it was until now. The thing that has always been missing is you. I so wish that we can share every holiday together. That I could wake up and have you there with me. Us cooking dinner and waiting for our family to come over so we can all break bread together. What could be better than that. I can't think of anything else...

Rest Well My Love

Your Future Husband

Day 62

Dear Future Wife

I struggle to write this today. I hate when I get in my feelings in times like this. I see so many out there experiencing what I should be experiencing. What have they done differently? I have witnessed so many happy unions of those that are near and dear to me and the comfort that is always provided is " Yours will be here soon" As if they know that E.T.A of you. I just want this to happen baby. I want to hold you. I want to kiss you. I want to be able to tell you each and every day how much I love you because there would be no doubt that I did. I'm not good with patience but I'm trying to develop it for you. I am trying to wait and trust that you are being prepared for me. But it's hard. I can't sleep right now because I need you here next to me. My heart is heavy and I don't know how to fix it. I love you and I just want to be able to tell you for myself.

Your Future Husband

Day 63

Dear Future Wife

Today I am going to be a part of this dating auction a friend of mine is having. To be honest with you I am not really feeling up to it but I made a promise to be there so I am going to keep my word.

I have never been to anything like this before. So I really don't know what to expect. My brother said " hey maybe you will find your future wife there" What if what he said is true? How will I know it's you? What sign will you present that tells me that it's you and my search is over. I am sitting here racking my brain right now because of the possibility of you being there. I am ready... I'm going to go in here with the faith that my prayers will be answered. I hope to see you soon

Your Future Husband

Day 64

Dear Future Wife

Do you want up reaching for me? Do you look on the other side of the bed and wish that I was laying there? How does it make you feel when you realize that it was just a dream? Baby I swear my dreams of you have been so real. I feel everything. I smell everything. I taste everything, but then I wake up and it's all gone. How cruel this all feels right now. I'm so tired of just dreaming of you. I need to live those dreams right now.

Your Future Husband

Day 65

Dear Future Wife

I met someone that resembles everything I prayed for in you but I am unsure if she is. I don't want to rush into thinking that she is the one but I will tell you that there is some excitement there. It was in the initial first look. Everything but her disappeared in the room we were in. When she spoke I had the feeling of DeJa Vu. I could've sworn I heard her voice before and that smile.... Baby if that's you then that's the smile I have dreamt of. I don't know what to make of all this.... I'm going to sleep on this....

I Love You

Your Future Husband

Day 66

Dear Future Wife

Is it natural to get lost in conversation. I swear right now that's what I am feeling. I have been having some amazing conversations about life and the future with the woman I spoke on that resembles you. She honestly makes me smile in every sense of the word.... She Makes Me Smile!!! I haven't been able to do that in so long. I wish I knew what this was. I wish I had the answer to if this is where I am supposed to be because right now I feel.....I feel..... I feel complete

Your Future Husband

Day 67

Dear Future Wife

I went and got some advice from a very good friend of mine about my last two entries. She told me if this woman displays everything I have been looking for and praying for then stop over thinking and just let it come naturally. She told me that I should start writing to her because if I don't speak it into existence it will never happen. God I want this to happen. I want her to be the one but I'm afraid.

Baby I hope it's you.

Goodnight Baby

Your Future Husband

Day 68

Dear Future Wife

About a month ago I announced that I was doing a Dear Future Husband competition. I was looking for a woman that could reflect what I write about. One that in one letter could capture and captivate my heart in such a way that God himself would tell me "She" is the one. I have gotten some really great entries but I think it's time to end the competition because I haven't found that letter. Now don't get me wrong because there are some amazing letters that I have read but I just haven't felt that there was one who topped them all. Maybe because it's not you writing it. I wonder what you would say. I wonder how much love would be displayed in your letter. I guess only time will tell. I love you

Your Future Husband

Day 69

Dear Future Wife

Now just when I went and opened my mouth about ending the competition in comes a letter from the woman that I have been speaking about in my last few letters. I let her read one of my letters and she responded because she felt inspired to. But baby everything.... and I do mean everything that she put in that letter knocked me off my feet. She spoke past my mind, past my heart, she spoke to my spirit. Could it be you? Baby are you finally here? I can't begin to tell you how happy I am right now. It's like she knew me without even knowing me. I keep telling myself to calm down but I feel like a kid in the candy store right now about to get my favorite candy. Let's see where this goes

Always Yours

Your Future Husband

Day 70

Dear Future Wife

This will probably be the hardest letter I ever write you. But I feel it needs to be written. They say the hardest part of the truth is having to face it. For 9 months there's a truth I hadn't faced even though I told myself constantly that I had. I'm afraid of you. Before you look to deep into it let me explain. I've been a product of pain my who life. Far too many times I've given myself completely to those I thought were meant to complete me. I placed all my trust in the unknown of them and completely let me guards down. Maybe that's where I went wrong. I was giving before I had any idea of who they were or what they were willing to give. A relationship is supposed to be a partnership, a 50\50 agreement that specifies if you're in it so am I. That there is no giving up on this. I got your back if you got mine. That I'd rather spend my whole life trying to get it right with you then look to another to be what you're destined to. But in each situation that wasn't the case. I was giving bits and pieces of me to everyone to the point where I can say that part of me that was together, that knew what I wanted, that was ready to go the extra mile and fight for love.... Yeah that part of me is broken. Writing that right now at this very moment hurts like hell. I mean was I not important enough to go the extra mile with? Was I not with fighting for? I thought that if I had everything together, that if I loved a woman with everything in me, if I catered to her every need that would be enough to make her see...... Me. I mean that's all I ever wanted was to be seen. It's hard being in a relationship and feel invisible. But I don't blame them, I blame me. If I couldn't recognize the worth in me how could anyone else see it. I lost me in the process of looking for what appeared to be you.

But if there's one thing I've learned in these past 9 months it's this..... Love Is Never Unsure. It's an abstract beauty that only true artist see and understand. The love I have to offer most will never understand. They will run from it or fear it without even taking the time to watch it develop. The most beautiful flowers start as seeds but if cared for properly they bloom beautifully. Why am I saying this? Why am I barring my soul in this letter? The answer is very simple..... I'm ready to bloom with you. Far to long have I been a withering vine. I'm ready to produce something beautiful. I'm ready to try with everything in me. I may be broken but with you I want to be whole again. I'm ready to remove the caution tape from around my heart and let you in. But baby I'm scared. Scared that I'll love you too hard. That I'll fail at being considerate of your feelings. That the fear of failure will rear its ugly head again. I will fear not being the perfect gentleman, not holding you tight enough, not helping you see how much you make my world spin. I went 30 years without you and now the only thought I want is spending the next 60 plus years making up for lost time. But I need something from you. When I want to run don't let me. When I get lost redirect me. When I can't see lead me. Remind me that we're in this together. Don't just pray for me pray with me. Be my shoulder. Hug me tighter. Be patient with me when patience is hard to find. Know that I am trying my hardest. More than anything else...... Just love me..... That's all I ask. I promise after its all said and done. When the lights go out. When the smoke clears I will be right by your side because you are the one woman who managed to truly unconditionally love me.

Yours Forever

Your Future Husband

After all the letters, after all the tears, after all the prayers. Love brought this letter from her..... Chanel Bean

Dear Future Husband

I need a man that sees the imperfections in me yet acknowledges my flaws and still accepts them all.
I need a man that truly understands that when I am not acting like myself I am simply scared.
I need him to grab my hand and let me know it's okay and that he will always be there.
To not just agree with me because of my physical beauty but look in my eyes and see the stories untold.
Cup his hands and catch my emotions if they over flow.
Not just discard me because he isn't getting exactly what he wants from me but understands that he is getting what he needs from me.

Letter's To My Future Wife

I want to become one with this man.
When I look in the mirror my reflection is him.
I want to speak as one be on the same accord.
I need a man that will force me to do better.
I want to upgrade myself every day as to where he will always want
to come home and never stray.
I need a man that understands the fear of losing me.
A man that I can build a family with.
Create life and share our morals and values.
Let live and let God. Hold hands in the park.
A kiss on the forehead every night as we slow dance to the rhythm
of our hearts.
I want this man to be my husband.
To wake everyday and see he is still next to me.
Appreciate me for my inner beauty and think of our intimacy as an
added bonus.
I want my husband to wipe my tears away.
Make me laugh so my fears depurate.
I want to cater to my husband.
Show him just how much love is harvested just for him.
I want to show him every day that I am grateful that I was the one
he chose.
A blessing God sent my way.
Rub his head when he has had a long day.
Massage his body to take the day's stress away.
I want to kiss him gently; sweet and sincere just to hear his sigh of
relief.
Silent prayers are sent to God's ears not to send him to me but to
prepare me once he finds me.

I want to be flawed and all and yet he falls for my true beauty.
Every day is a day to better myself for the man that is doing the same for me.
I am in a forever changing platform of life and the me right now may not be the woman he needs.
I want to fulfill his desires and put away his fears.
Help him embrace life. I want to be this man's wife and all that that in tells.
His pride and joy outside of our children. The reason he breathes life.
I need this man to come searching for me as I am for him.

I am lost until he is found.

Letter From The Author

I thank you for taking the time out to read this first edition of Letters To My Future Wife. Words can't begin to tell you just how grateful I am for all the love and support I have received in writing this book. To be totally honest this started and has always been my way of healing myself from the hurt I felt daily from not having the woman I wanted to spend my life with. I never expected it to touch anyone but I have witnessed it touch so many. I give all thanks to God for that. Without him there would be no me. To all my fans this is only the beginning. There are so many more letters on the way. I just feel that I want you to take a journey with me as I find out the plan God has for me and the woman he has created to be my wife. I can't say thank you enough. On those days where I lost faith, where I was emotionally drained, where nothing made sense it was your post that pushed me to keep going. To not lose sight of the ultimate goal. I don't know what the future holds as of right now but I do know that there is love in it for me and you. Never give up on your dreams, never stop praying, never stop believing because I can promise you your time will come. I am a walking testimony of that. This book is only a glimpse into my life. I am a work in progress but I can assure you when it's all said and done I will be a beautiful piece of work. To My Future Wife I thank you for everything you have given me in the search for you. The Best Is Yet To Come!!!!

Sincerely
Your Future Husband

Letter's To My Future Wife

Made in the USA
San Bernardino, CA
23 February 2020